I Can Run

Written by Gay Su Pinnell
Illustrated by Melissa Sweet

SCHOLASTIC INC.
New York   Toronto   London   Auckland   Sydney
Mexico City   New Delhi   Hong Kong   Buenos Aires

I can .

run

I can  .

run

I can  .

swim

4

I can .

swim

I can .

jump

I can  .

jump

I can  .

sleep

8

I can .

sleep

Text copyright © 2002 by Scholastic Inc.
Illustrations copyright © 2002 by Melissa Sweet.
All rights reserved. Published by Scholastic Inc.
Printed in the U.S.A.

ISBN 0-439-53346-5

7   8   9   10   23   12 11 10 09 08 07 06 05